PSALM TWENTY-THREE

PSALM TWENTY-THREE

A Devotional

by

HADDON W. ROBINSON

MOODY PRESS • CHICAGO

ISBN 0-8024-6935-3

Twelfth Printing, 1982

To My Father, and My
Parents in Love
Who Love the Shepherd Dearly

MEET THE SHEPHERD

THE TWENTY-THIRD PSALM stands as the classic song of the Psalter. Though of ancient origin, like all great classics it does not wear out. John Keats assures us that:

> A thing of beauty is a joy forever:
> Its loveliness increases; it will never
> Pass into nothingness.

Literary critics value the Twenty-third Psalm as a masterpiece of lyric poetry. But this exquisite little psalm has not won its place in our hearts because of scholars' praise. Common people everywhere have received it gladly. At first thought, it might surprise us that they should do so. In general, the unliterary man does not read poetry. If he does, it is the simple, easily understood proverb about life published in the evening newspaper.

Understanding the Twenty-third Psalm does not come that easily. Its imagery conceals as well as reveals, and not every commentator interprets it the same way. For some it is all about sheep and their shepherd, but others insist that only the first three verses talk about sheep. The last three verses, they feel, describe a dinner guest with his host. Still others feel that there are three pictures in the psalm: a shepherd with his sheep (vv. 1-2), a guide and a traveler (vv. 3-4) and a host entertaining his guest (vv. 5-6). If scholars disagree, we might suppose that ordinary men would throw up their hands in defeat. They do not.

Understanding the Twenty-third Psalm could be difficult because its imagery is distant from the experiences of modern man. God is compared to a weather-driven shepherd. To appreciate this metaphor we must leave the surroundings of our air-conditioned houses and live under the blaze of a Syrian sun. "The LORD is my shepherd; I shall not want." Communication might improve if we paraphrased it, "The Lord is my mechanic; he keeps me in repair." That, of course, would ruin it. To the Palestinian shepherd sheep were more than a commodity.

In our impersonal, machine-centered age we appreciate these words because they are personal. God takes the same patient, unwearying care of His people as a shepherd of his flock. God's concern for individuals is clearly evident in the psalm.

Leon Bloy, the French poet and mystic, once described his writings by saying, "I am simply a poor man who seeks his God, sobbing and calling him along all roads." His was a personal search, but this psalm goes beyond that.

The Twenty-third Psalm is the affirmation of a profound, personal faith in God. The theologian defines God as: "A spirit—infinite, eternal and unchangeable; in his being are wisdom, power, holiness, justice, goodness and truth." This is as cold and impersonal as a dictionary. But the Twenty-third Psalm shows theology in action in the life of a man like ourselves. It reveals the God of personal experience.

We can identify with the author of the Twenty-third Psalm. The heading tells us that we are reading "A Psalm of David." Although some critics strongly disagree, recent evidence from the archaeological site in Syria, Ras Shamra, supports the historical reliability of these ascriptions. More important, Christ and the apostles considered them part of the Scriptures.

When you receive a letter, you glance first at the signature to see who wrote it. When you browse through a new book, you look at the dust jacket to get some background on the author. While it may not be indispensable to the understanding of a writing, knowing the author provides important clues.

Since this is David's song we know that his expression of trust is not the carefree unconcern of a child. David was a mature man, filled with his share of the conflicting passions and confusing problems that confront any human being. Not only was he the heroic slayer of Goliath, the devoted friend of Jonathan, a lover of music and an able king, but he was also a haggard fugitive, an adulterer and a murderer. He slew his enemies as any ancient monarch did, but when Saul became an unrelenting enemy, David took only Saul's shield when he could have taken his life. As a father, he had watched his baby die, and had wept when Absalom, an ungrateful son, was slain as he led an armed rebellion against his father. David has not left us with only "beautiful thoughts," but with an honest testimony about God learned while living life to the hilt.

As a result, though this psalm is distant from our times, its lessons are still appropriate. As the Quakers used to say, it "speaks to our condition." "The meaning and helpfulness of this perfect little Psalm can never be exhausted," Professor W. T. Davison declares, "so long as men, like sheep, wander and need guidance, and so long as they learn to find it in God their shepherd."

Admittedly, we live in complex times, but the Shepherd of whom the psalmist wrote has not changed. Perhaps, to our loss, you and I have become too sophisticated to trust Him. Faith appears too simple for twentieth century living.

A woman complained to her pastor, "I don't know what it means to trust."

He responded, "Tell me, did you ever learn to float?"

"Well, I've *tried* to," she answered.

The pastor drove home his point. "Isn't that exactly the reason that you didn't succeed? If you want to float, you must let the water bear you up. The water will do its part if you will let it!"

As one sheep to another, therefore, I commend this well-loved psalm and its Shepherd to you for your complete trust.

HADDON W. ROBINSON

FREE FROM WANT

It has been noted that every major portion of Scripture was written *by* someone having a hard time, *to* men and women experiencing a hard time. This may not be exactly true, but I do know that the passages of Scripture we love best are the ones to which we turn in days of difficulty. And no passage in all the Book of God is any better loved or any more familiar than the Twenty-third Psalm.

The words of the psalm were not penned during the morning of David's life, nor the noontime of his experience. I believe they were written during David's twilight years, for they are the words of a man who has lived and done much, who has greatly sinned and been greatly forgiven.

David is an old man who rules as king in Jerusalem. As he sits upon his throne, memory comes and takes him by the hand and leads him back to his yesterdays. Suddenly the great vaulted arches of his palace disappear and in their place he sees again the azure blue of a Mediterranean sky. The scepter that he holds in his hand becomes a shepherd's crook. And the great, thick rugs beneath his feet are as the grassy pastures he trod so often as a boy. As David looks out at his servants standing around his throne, eager to do his bidding, they appear now like the flock that he cared for on his father's farm. David remembers how he cared for the flock, how he led the sheep to places of plenty and protected them from danger. Then as David sighs for those "good old days" he begins to think of how God has taken care of him—how God has provided for his needs and protected him from danger. Inspired by the Spirit, David writes, "The LORD is my shepherd; I shall not want."

Many who love this psalm take these words to mean "The Lord is my Saviour; and I'm glad He is." As wonderful as it is to know that Jesus is your Saviour, that is not what this psalm is all about. Psalm 23 is one of a trilogy of psalms that appear together in the Psalter: Psalms 22, 23 and 24. Each deals with a different aspect of the work of Christ. Psalm 22 sketches a prophetic picture of the death of Christ upon the cross. In it David stares down across the hills of history and sees the knoll of Calvary with the suffering Messiah hanging on a tree. Psalm 23, however, deals with the resurrected Christ, who is now in heaven. Psalm 24 speaks of the triumphant Christ who shall return to earth. "Lift up your heads, O ye gates, and be ye lift up, ye everlasting doors; and the King of glory shall come in. Who is this King of glory? The LORD of hosts, he is the King of glory" (vv. 7, 10).

Psalm 22 delivers me from the *penalty* of my sin. Through Christ's death my debt of sin is paid and I know that God will not hold it against me. If my Saviour has paid the penalty, then of course I have nothing to pay. Through Him I enter into life. Psalm 23 delivers me from the *power* of sin. As I trust my life into the hands of the Christ who now lives for me, I am assured that every need of every day in every circumstance can be supplied. In Him I enjoy an abundant life. Psalm 24 delivers me from the *presence* of sin. It points forward to that delightful day when Christ shall return for His own, and with Him we shall share life for eternity.

Psalm 22 took place in the past, and it takes care of my past; Psalm 23 takes place in the present, and it guarantees my present; Psalm 24 will take place in the future, and it assures my future. Psalm 22 deals with the "good shepherd" who "giveth his life for the sheep" (John 10:11). Psalm 23 deals with the "great shepherd" resurrected for the sheep (Heb. 13:20). Psalm 24 deals with the "chief Shepherd" who returns to reward His sheep (I Peter 5:4). Many people who have put their trust in Christ as Saviour do not know the reality of His work as Shepherd and do not look forward to His return as Sovereign. But when David sang of Christ as Shepherd, he was praising the living God who enriched his daily life, who would send Christ as Messiah and who would give him eternal life.

This word that David used for "LORD" was the name "Yahweh." The Jewish people were so much in awe of that name—and of the God it represented—that they substituted for it some lesser name for God whenever it occurred in the public reading of the Scriptures. In fact, only once a year was it pronounced, on the Day of Atonement, by the high priest in the most holy place of the temple. This superstition grew out of a misunderstanding of Leviticus 24:16: "And he that blasphemeth the name of the LORD, he shall surely be put to death." When people thought of Yahweh, they thought of the One who causes all things to be, the God who brought the nation Israel into existence. Yet this God who inhabits eternity is the one that David speaks of as "shepherd." He is the God that Christians trust too. The Christ in whom we trust as a personal Saviour is the same One by whom and through whom and for whom all things were made. That God is great enough to take care of all the needs of my life. That God visited this planet and died on the cross for man's sin. It is this great God whose return we look for, and it is Yahweh, revealed in Jesus Christ, that we trust for life itself in time and in eternity.

Another important word in that first verse is the tiny personal pronoun *my*. Millions of people know that the Lord is *a* Shepherd, but they really don't know that He is *theirs*. How can you know that you are really one of His sheep, and that the God of the universe is actually *your* Shepherd? Well, in John 10:27 Christ Himself declared, "My sheep hear my voice, and I know them, and they follow me: and I give unto them eternal life; and they shall never perish, neither shall any man pluck them out of my hand."

There are two tests. "My sheep hear my voice," He said. That's the first one. Do you really listen to what He has to say to you through His Word? Then He said, "They follow me." That's the second test. They carefully follow the leadership that He gives them in His Word. It's as simple—and as sublime—as that.

Who is your shepherd? Your husband or wife? Your pastor? Your parent? Your psychologist? A close friend? As important as these people are, they can never be the Good Shepherd of your life. They're sheep too. You and they need someone else just as David did. You can have someone else—if you give attention to what He says in His Word and simply follow His instructions. When you come to the place where all of your life—in all of its details—is placed in Christ's care, you can say with a deep, abiding certainty, "The LORD is *my* shepherd; I shall not want."

ACCEPT WITH JOY

W HEN MY YOUNGSTERS were growing up, I used to ask them, "If you could become an animal, what kind of animal would you choose to be?" My daughter usually wanted to be a soft, purring kitten, or a mink so she would have a built-in fur coat. My small son would rather have been an elephant so that he could squirt water through his nose. In all the times we have played our game, however, neither of them has ever decided to be a sheep.

My children are not very different from the great nations, are they? The United States regards a gallant eagle as its national symbol. Great Britain has its lion. Russia has the bear. As far as I know, no nation has ever adopted the emblem of a sheep. In fact, we were insulted, or should have been, when a recent book called us *A Nation of Sheep.*

A sheep is all of the things that we do not want to be. It is defenseless, dependent and stupid. But when David wrote, "The LORD is my shepherd; I shall not want," he was also saying by implication that he was a sheep—he was defenseless, dependent and foolish. You and I might as well admit it: Before God, we too are sheep. Yet in the depths of our proud hearts that is a very difficult admission to make.

You will never be able to appreciate the Twenty-third Psalm unless you realize that David is writing from the viewpoint of a sheep. And you will never enter into its blessings unless you will admit that you are really a sheep yourself. Because the psalmist allowed the Lord to be His Shepherd, he did not want. The phrase, "I will not want" should probably be translated, "I am never in a state of want." In other words, "Because the Lord is my Shepherd I shall never want at any time for anything I need." This is the key to the whole psalm.

David is writing about his relationship to a wonderful Person. Sometimes, though, we get so taken up with the details of this psalm that we actually ignore the Shepherd. We are delighted at the prospect of green pastures and quiet waters. We respond to the promise of an overflowing cup. Indeed, we are so eager for all the Shepherd does, we do not pay much attention to who the Shepherd is. Yet He is at the center of the entire psalm. All of these blessings are mine because I am one of His sheep. It reminds me of a string of pearls—the pearls do not look like much unless they are held together by the string. And the person of the Lord Jesus Christ—whom we must trust as our Shepherd—runs throughout this entire psalm.

Dr. Van Gilder in one of his comments on the psalm said that there may come a time when you will be sitting under the shade tree of blessings, and the winds of adversity will rage in your sky and rip that tree up by its roots. Or there may come a time when you will be grazing in the pastures of plenty and the sun of trouble will arise and burn to the roots the grass on which you have been feeding. And at a time like that you will need a Shepherd. For the sheep's eyes are too filled with tears, and its heart is too filled with fear for it to find the way itself. You will need a Shepherd to take you to new pastures and to find for you new shade trees under which you can rest. In this case the gift without the Giver is not only worthless, it is impossible.

David says that if the Lord is your Shepherd, every area and activity of your life is under His direction and protection and control. Donald Oakley in his helpful little booklet, *For Sheep Only*, asks the question, "Should sheep complain?" Complaining has become a fine talent in modern life. We can excuse it by saying that it is a safety valve which lets off the pressure of pent-up resentment and frustration. Maybe so. But is this the mark of a sheep? Should a Christian complain? When he does, he is saying that he does not have what he wants, does not like his situation, and the whole thing is not quite fair. But the psalmist declares, "The LORD is my shepherd; I shall not want." Often we can quote the first half of this phrase, but when it comes to trusting our Shepherd and His sufficiency in all our "wants" and needs, we fail miserably. We are unwilling to accept trials and testings as part of daily living. We may act patient and kind, but we fume inside with anger and discontent.

When we get an unpleasant job to do, we think in our hearts, "What a raw deal, but I'm not going to complain. I'm a Christian and I'm not supposed to." Or when someone else is in the limelight as a result of our work, we sulk in the corner. "There he is getting all the credit when I'm the one who did the work, but I'll control myself because I'm a good Christian." Perhaps what we need is to be able to look at life as David did. He believed that the Lord really was his Shepherd—and I must trust that too. David also believed that the Lord planned his life down to the details of his day, as a good Shepherd would. In this knowledge we can learn to accept His will with joy, believing that these trials and testings are part of His plan for us. Moreover, I must believe that He is able and willing to help me do what He has planned for me today. That is part of a shepherd's work for his sheep. He certainly would not lead me to a difficult circumstance and run off and leave me. Only a hireling would do something like that! In this assurance, I can even accept personal injustices and be at peace in my heart.

When the Jewish people—over whom David ruled as king—complained in the wilderness, they were judged. The writer of Hebrews said that their complaining was a symptom of unbelief. A lack of trust in the Shepherd. I wonder what our complaining is a symptom of. Why not admit that you are merely a sheep in need of a Shepherd's guidance and care. Then if you admit this, trust your life into His hands. Just leave it there, and accept His direction and selection of events. Let each difficulty become an opportunity to see Him at work in your life. He has said, "I will never leave thee nor forsake thee." If you are one of His flock, you can count on that. When you do, I believe you will sing with the psalmist: The Lord is my Shepherd; I am never in any want.

REST OF SPIRIT

THREE THOUSAND YEARS have passed since the Psalmist David first sang the words of the Twenty-third Psalm. The sand of those thirty centuries has buried beneath it many of the relics of that distant day. The harp on which this ancient melody was played, the book of the law from which King David drew his meditations, the royal chamber in which the psalmist composed his song, are now all covered with the debris of the ages. Yet, the Twenty-third Psalm is still as fresh as the day it was first composed. Its ancient words are among the first that many of us learned as children. They are often among the last that we whisper to loved ones who lie in the darkness of life waiting for the daybreak of heaven. The sufferer in the hospital room, the soldier at his lonely post, the stranger in a distant land, men burdened down with iron cares, many have been encouraged by these words. Only God Himself knows how often the Twenty-third Psalm has encouraged those who were dying and comforted those who were left behind.

In this pastoral symphony, the first verse sounds the theme of the psalm. If the Lord is our Shepherd, we will not want. In coming to trust *who* the Shepherd is, we can come to appreciate *what* the Shepherd does. For example, if the Lord really is your Shepherd and you are really one of His sheep, you will not want for rest. He makes His sheep to lie down in green pastures.

Sheep are rather stupid animals. In fact, some commentators insist that the only reason God ever bothered to create sheep at all was to have an illustration of what Christians are like. That is a bit farfetched, I'm sure, but it is true that often sheep, like people, do not know when to rest. At times when a flock should be resting in preparation for a difficult trek lying before them, something will excite them. Perhaps it will be the growl of a mountain lion, or the bark of a dog, or merely the shout of a child. Yet this can bother the sheep and drive them to running back and forth across the pasture.

The wise shepherd knows that the sheep have need of rest; therefore, he will move into the midst of the flock and, catching a sheep, he will gently force it to lie down and feed quietly on the cool, green grass. He makes his sheep to lie down in green pastures. We live in a hectic, hurried, harassed age in which headache medicine has become the national beverage. Sometimes we find it almost impossible to rest. *Time* magazine reports that the American public gulps down tons of sleeping pills trying to get a little rest—but the next day we are back in the same maddening pace, racing around in circles and wearing ourselves out. We would like to rest, of course, but somehow we fear that if we really did take time out to lie down, it would be so hard to catch up with the crowd again that it would hardly be worth the trouble. And even when we stop running, the tensions under which we live are so tight that we feel the need for rest even when we are trying to relax. Weekend neurotics, for example, worry that they will not be able to squeeze all the fun they can out of their playtime.

When the Shepherd steps into this situation He often forces us to rest. Your "green pastures" may actually be a hospital bed of white, but sometimes God makes us rest even when we do not want to. God gives us much more than physical rest: He gives us rest of spirit. No part of our nature cries more urgently for rest than our inner being. The book of Hebrews says that one of the things God does for His own is to give them rest. When a man comes to trust Christ completely he can act upon God's promises and respond eagerly to God's command. Life is simplified when we have only one Person to please and only one Master to serve. Leaving all of life's choices with the Shepherd, we find rest.

It is possible for many of us, because of our unbelief, to be in the midst of green pastures and fail to recognize them. We look at the circumstances into which our Shepherd may have led us, but we fail to see them from His viewpoint. Our eyes may be on the dirt, and we fail to see the green grass that is growing there for our benefit. Do you remember when Peter was thrown into prison by King Herod? Just a short while earlier this same king had thrown James, another disciple, into the same prison and had him executed. Peter had no reason to believe that the king would do anything different with him. Peter, however, was lying in the prison cell asleep. In the face of Herod's sword, he was very much at rest. Apparently Peter knew that even a prison cell can be a green pasture in which to rest—when your Shepherd has led you there.

Do not misunderstand. Peter knew he was in prison. He was not a bright eyed mystic that thought of a prison cell as a comfortable living room. He did not get rest by fooling himself into thinking that the circumstances were better than they were. Peter trusted the Shepherd—he knew His goodness. He did not doubt that his Shepherd could guarantee his safety and provide all that was best for him even in a dungeon. When you trust the shepherd *that* way, you can find rest for your soul and sleep for your body. But this rest comes only to those who are Christ's sheep.

God wants to be appropriated. There is a great difference between knowledge and appropriation. A tourist stands and looks at a lovely home. He says, "It's a beautiful house." A man standing next to him says, "Yes, it is. It's *mine!*"

It makes all the difference whether you can say, "Jesus is a Saviour" or "Jesus has saved me." And it makes all the difference between life and life abundant whether you can say the Lord is *a* Shepherd or the Lord is *your* Shepherd. Jesus Christ wants to be appropriated. He is not content to be a Shepherd, a good Shepherd, or the Shepherd of angels. He will never be satisfied—and neither will you—until from the depths of your soul, and in the reality of your experience, you can say, "He is mine!" When you can say this, you will know His rest. You will discover, as David did, that He leads His sheep to rest in green pastures.

WHEN BANNERS DROOP

My PARENTS came from Scotland and Ireland, where it has been a custom for congregations to sing psalms. My parents sometimes sang a psalm as they worked. Most often it was this version of the Twenty-third Psalm:

> The Lord's my Shepherd, I'll not want; He makes me down to
>   lie
> In pastures green; He leadeth me the quiet waters by.
> My soul He doth restore again; and me to walk doth make
> Within the paths of righteousness, e'en for His own name's
>   sake.
> Yea, though I walk through death's dark vale, yet will I
>   fear no ill;
> For Thou art with me, and Thy rod and staff me comfort still.
> My table Thou has furnished in presence of my foes;
> My head Thou dost with oil anoint, and my cup overflows.
> Goodness and mercy all my life shall surely follow me;
> And in God's house forevermore my dwelling place shall be.

It is a great song because it is a great psalm. Yet to many thousands of people this psalm is little more than poetry, containing little more reality in their experience than a nursery rhyme. Such people know the psalm, but they do not know the Shepherd. When David wrote these words he was describing reality—something that was taking place in the twists and turns of daily living. David knew God as Shepherd just as we may know Christ as Shepherd. He could testify that if the Lord is your Shepherd you will not want. The sheep who trust the Shepherd will not want for rest because He makes them to lie down in green pastures. In addition, Christ's sheep will not want for refreshment because He leads His flock beside the still waters.

This word for "still waters" could be translated "stilled waters." As in most of this psalm, David is thinking of an incident that occurs in the shepherd life of Palestine. Sheep are deeply afraid of running water. Instinctively they seem to realize that if water should get on their coats of wool, they would become waterlogged and sink beneath a stream. As a result, a flock tired and thirsty after making a difficult journey over the blistering sands will come to a running stream. The cool, crystal clear waters can quench the thirst of the weary animals, but the sheep will only stand beside the stream and look. Fear of the water keeps them from refreshment. Then the shepherd, taking his rod and staff, pries loose a few large stones and dams up a quiet place where the sheep may drink. In the midst of a rushing stream, he provides refreshment for the flock with water that he has stilled.

Has your Shepherd ever done this for you? Has it ever seemed to you that the circumstances of life were more than you could bear? Have you ever drawn back in fear when it seemed that life, like a rampaging stream, would suck you under and bury you beneath its flow? All of us, I suppose, have experienced times like that. How often, at such times, we Christians whisper to ourselves that "all things work together for good to them that love God, to them who are the called according to his purpose." But even while we repeat those words of Romans 8:28 we are afraid. Then our Shepherd comes, and with His rod and staff He works through those events that we feared most and makes them a source of spiritual refreshment. Many of us can look back on days that made us afraid and say from the depths of our souls, "Those were the good days, when we received spiritual refreshment from the hand of our Shepherd." We received this refreshment from the circumstances that we dreaded most.

One thing we may discover when the Shepherd ministers to us is that we are often afraid of things that are not really there. We hear the rush of the stream and see the splashing waters, and we draw back in fear because of imagined dangers. Like children in the dark, we are sometimes more fearful of the shadows than we would ever be of the reality. Of course, our Shepherd not only leads us to the waters that He has stilled, but if our imagery is correct, He also leads us beside the rushing stream. Do you think that He would lead His flock to a place like that if He did not also plan to provide the protection and provision that they need?

Martha Snell Nicholson, never strong as a child, suffered a complete breakdown in early womanhood. She was in bed over seven years—years of endless waiting, of pain and weakness of body that almost crushed her brave spirit within. Then after a partial recovery came a series of difficult operations which seemed to do little good. In her last years she was in constant pain and in increasing weakness. Through all this time she wrote poetry that set forth the ministry of her Shepherd in the sickroom. Thus she made fruitful those weary years that others might have found completely barren. One day Mrs. Nicholson's physician told her that her case was too far advanced to respond to treatment. In that hour of weariness she wrote this poem titled "When He Putteth Forth His Own Sheep He Goeth Before Them."

I could not walk this darkening path of pain alone;
The years have taken toll of me;
Sometimes my banners droop; my arms have grown too tired,
And laughter comes less easily.
And often these—my shrinking cowardly eyes refuse
To face the thing ahead of me,
The certainty of growing pain and helplessness . . .
But oh, my Lord is good, for He
Comes quickly to me as I lie there in the dust
Of my defeat and shame and fear;
He stoops and raises me and sets me on my feet,
And softly whispers in my ear
That He will never leave me—nay, that He will go
Before me all the way. And so,
My hand in His, along this brightening path of pain,
My Lord and I go together.

RESTORED TO FELLOWSHIP

If I BELIEVED the way you do," I overheard one of my friends saying, "I'd become a Christian and then go out and have a wild time." Sitting across the table from him and adding fuel to a fiery debate on eternal security, another friend defended the position: "Once a Christian, always a Christian." Going to an extreme, however, he was actually in danger of saying that a person could be a Christian no matter how he conducted his daily life.

"Then why not really live it up," his opponent countered, "if you're dead certain that you can never lose your salvation?"

I had a hard time keeping out of the argument at that point. My friend was a Christian. Was he actually saying that he would prefer to belong to Christ yet still live like the devil? Seemingly both friends were missing the truth that Christianity is a relationship with the most wonderful Person in the universe, Jesus Christ. That relationship is such a dynamic one that David could say in Psalm 23, "The LORD is my shepherd; I shall not want." As a sheep is constantly in a shepherd's care, David declares a believer is in the constant care of the Lord. This relationship should make a difference in the way we live. In fact, enjoying a relationship like that makes the old life quite dull.

If we really belong to Him, attractions of another sheepfold will not steal our heart. The sheep who follow the Shepherd, Jesus Christ, know that their Shepherd not only provides rest in making them to lie down in green pastures, and refreshment in leading them beside the still waters, but they realize, as David did, that Christ restores His sheep when they wander.

Sheep have a habit of wandering away from the flock. Often a sheep becomes interested in one clump of grass—and then another and another—until finally it looks up to discover that it has strayed far away from the shepherd and the other sheep. When night comes the lost sheep is in great danger. Lurking in the darkness are small wolves eager to pounce upon it and rip it apart. Or, unable to see its way, the sheep may fall over the side of a cliff. When the shepherd comes back to the fold at night he counts his sheep, calling each one by name to be sure it is in its place. When he discovers that one of the sheep is still out in the wild, he leaves his flock in the care of a trusted servant and trudges back over the route that he and the flock traveled that day. He carries a small lantern down close to his feet as he retraces his steps. Calling out to his sheep, he listens for its bleating in the darkness. When he finds the animal, he places it upon his shoulders and carries it back to the sheepfold.

Occasionally a sheep will develop a habit of going astray. Every evening when the shepherd counts the flock he finds the same sheep missing. Night after night, he goes out seeking the lost animal. After this has occurred several times, the shepherd will once more go out to find the sheep, but this time before carrying it back to the fold, he will break its leg. Back in the fold the shepherd makes a splint for the shattered leg and, during the days that follow, he carries that crippled sheep close to his heart. As the leg begins to mend, the shepherd sets the sheep down by his side. To the crippled animal, the smallest stream looms like a giant river, the tiniest knoll rises like a mountain. The sheep depends completely upon the shepherd to carry it across the terrain. After the leg has healed the sheep has learned a lesson: It must stay close to the shepherd's side.

Many feel that it is an act of cruelty for a shepherd to break the leg of a poor, defenseless sheep. It seems hardhearted, almost vicious, until you understand the shepherd's heart. Then you realize that what seems to be cruelty is really kindness. The shepherd knows that the sheep must remain close to him if it is to be protected from danger. So he breaks its leg, not to hurt it, but to restore it.

Have you ever had the experience of wandering away from God, forcing Him to suddenly move in and break your leg? Perhaps at that time when you were under the discipline of the Shepherd, you felt that He was too severe and too harsh. But when you know the Shepherd's purposes for you, you realize that these afflictions come into your life because He wants His sheep to depend constantly on Him. Notice that the text says *He* restores our soul. It is the work of the shepherd to go out and find the sheep that has strayed and bring it back.

David felt the heartache and heart healing of such an experience. He was guilty of sexual looseness with the beautiful Bathsheba. What is more, he tried to cover his sin by having her soldier husband, Uriah, killed in battle. It was planned, premeditated murder. David lived with the guilty memory of his sins for almost a year. His child was born to Bathsheba. In all this time it seemed that no one had found out his sin. Then God sent the Prophet Nathan to David with a simple story about a man who had a whole flock of sheep and his poor neighbor who had just one little lamb. The wealthy neighbor took the lamb from the poor farmer and killed it for a feast. David was incensed and swore that whoever had done this would be severely punished. Nathan the prophet pointed his finger at King David, and said, "Thou art the man."

In Psalm 51 you can read David's heart-cry to God when he confessed his sin to his Shepherd. We must remember, though, that before David ever sought the face of God the faithful Shepherd had sought out the wandering sheep. This is one of the ways we can be sure that we belong to Him—He has promised to restore His sheep when they wander. When you are out of fellowship with God, God seeks you out to draw you back to Himself. Or, to use another illustration, God disciplines the children in His family. The author of Hebrews says, "My son, despise not thou the chastening of the Lord, nor faint when thou art rebuked of Him; for whom the Lord loveth he chasteneth, and scourgeth every son whom he receiveth. . . . God dealeth with you as with sons; for what son is he whom the father chasteneth not" (Heb. 12:5-6). Though chastening is never enjoyable at the time, it is profitable, this passage goes on to explain, because it produces righteousness in our lives. Through it we are restored not only to fellowship with God but to a pattern of living that pleases Him.

ALONG RIGHT PATHS

MANY AUTHORS have looked at human beings as weary travelers journeying across a great expanse of wilderness called life. A thousand voices and a thousand paths constantly beckon us to go first one way and then another. For the most part we wander on in bewilderment, slipping into the first path that attracts us for the moment. When we discover that it ends in rocks and thickets, we back off and desperately try another one. "If only I knew what to do" is one of the most common expressions wrung from human hearts. Life for many people is like a map without any town names or route numbers. Seeking to find our way unguided is both difficult and dangerous.

Yet millions of people throughout the centuries have testified that in the midst of such uncertainty they have known the guidance of God. One such man speaks to us from Psalm 23. David was a man of many trades. As he grew up he was a farmer who took care of sheep. Then rapidly he rose to prominence in the land of Israel as a warrior, then as the noted leader of a mighty nation. As a farmer, a politician and a soldier, he lived with the dismay and the bewilderments of life common to us all. But he testifies, "The LORD is my Shepherd; I shall not want [for guidance]."

"He leadeth me in the paths of righteousness for his name's sake" (v. 3*b*). The phrase in the Hebrew is more clearly translated, "He leads me in the right paths." Once more this picture is drawn from shepherd life in Palestine, where many paths sprawl across the terrain. Some have been worn by travelers going from city to city. Others by robbers who want to lead a flock aside to attack the shepherd and steal his sheep. Still other paths have been made by the winds that have blown across the sand. To the untrained eye they all look like real paths. But when you follow them they lead nowhere.

David asserts that because the Lord is his Shepherd, he will not want for guidance because "He leads me in the right paths." When God leads us in the right paths He not only directs us to the right places, but He leads us to the right kind of life. When it comes to making decisions we often want to know only where God wants us to be. Whether it is in Dallas or Chicago, Africa or South America. But God's direction and leading is not so much to a place as to a position and character.

Some time ago I was faced with a rather difficult decision. Five different opportunities lay before me, and as I stood at the crossroads, forced to decide which path—if any—I should take, I was bewildered. God appeared to be saying, "There are five roads. Now find the right one." Turning to the Scriptures, I found this verse in Psalm 23 and was delighted to discover that God was not only willing but able to guide me and help me make my decision. But then as I began to look through the rest of the Bible to learn more about God's guidance, I discovered that the emphasis is not on *where* God wants me to be. I do not know of any verse that will tell me whether I should attend college next year or take that new job or move up North or come down South. I found instead that God's will concerns *what* He wants me to be.

Would you like to know God's will for your life today? Although I do not know you I can tell you what it is. For example, His will for you, we are told in the New Testament, is that you "in everything give thanks" (I Thess. 5:18). Or again the Apostle Paul tells us that God's will for us is our sanctification, that is, He desires that we be set apart for a holy purpose (I Thess. 4:3).

After I discovered that God's guidance has to do with *what* I am, not *where* I am, I realized that if I was what God wanted me to be, He would then place me where He wanted me. As long as I was walking with Him and allowing His Spirit to live His life through me, I did not have to be plagued by decisions. I could trust these things into the hands of God knowing that He could lead me to the place of His choosing.

Sometimes we get the impression that God has lost our address, that somehow we have been put aside in the shuffle and God no longer knows where we are or what we are doing. Of course that is not true. The Shepherd knows His sheep by name, and He knows both His purpose for them and their potential. He will see to it that the sheep who hear His voice and follow Him are where they ought to be.

Notice David says, "He leadeth me." We might want to emphasize the word *He*, because David is telling us that this leading grows out of a personal relationship. God does not give us a set of directions and tell us to follow them, but He Himself goes before us and takes us to the place of His choosing. He does not give us good directions; He gives us His own guidance. Shepherds in Palestine had a unique way of getting the sheep to follow them. As they strolled down a lane, they took their staff and reached up to a high limb where delicious fruit hung. Picking the fruit, they held it in their hand while they walked quietly on. The sheep, interested in getting the tasty tidbit, would crowd in close behind the shepherd and nibble at the fruit. Thus the shepherd led them as he fed them.

One of the ways God leads His sheep is by feeding them. God works through His Word to show us His will. We feed upon this Book and study it, and the Holy Spirit opens it and speaks to our hearts and shows us what He wants us to do. There is a direct relationship between feeding on the Word and the leading of the Shepherd.

Why does the Shepherd become so concerned with us? How can we be certain that we can trust His guidance? Notice the words, "He leadeth me . . . for his name's sake." The shepherd has a reputation to maintain. If a shepherd were to take a flock out into the wilderness and lose that flock to the wolves or lead them down wrong paths so that they could not find their way back home, he would be disgraced. He would be scorned in his community; no one would trust other sheep into his care. We can trust God, the Good Shepherd who will not lead men astray. It is for the sake of His character, for the sake of His name, that He leads safely home all the sheep that put their trust in Him.

SCHOOLROOM OF SUFFERING

CHAT WITH THE MAN next to you on a plane, or talk to your barber, or visit with your neighbor next door, and you discover that people are afraid. Most of us are afraid of tomorrow. Afraid that we may lose our jobs—or that we may have to keep them. Afraid that a certain candidate will not get elected—or that he will. Afraid that the youngsters may turn out wrong—or, if they grow up, that they may be blown up in a war. Afraid to live and afraid to die. We do not know what lies just over the hill. Terrible things are happening in our world and we are afraid.

Yet a Christian should not live in fear. In Psalm 23:4, David cries: "Yea, though I walk through the valley of the shadow of death, I will fear no evil: for thou art with me." The psalmist is simply saying: If the Lord is your Shepherd and you are His sheep, you will not want for courage even if you have to go through the most difficult places of life.

When we think of a valley we usually imagine a pleasant lowland sweep bounded by sloping hillsides. But the word for "valley" that the psalmist uses refers to a dreadful place—a home for vultures by day and a haven for wolves and hyenas by night. Moreover, instead of our translation "shadow of death," it would probably be more accurate to translate the phrase, "the valley of deep darkness." For the valley that the psalmist pictures is an actual place in Palestine—a chasm among the hills, a deep, abrupt, faintly lighted ravine with steep sides and a narrow floor.

Notice how verse 4 is related to verse 3. In verse 3 the psalmist declares, "He leads me in the right paths for His name's sake." Then, verse 4 is saying, "But one of the paths through which the Shepherd takes the sheep is the ravine of deep darkness."

Early in the year, the flocks graze in the lowlands, but as the summer comes and the hot sun melts the snows on the mountainsides, the shepherd leads his flock to the better grazing land on the mountains high above. In order to take the flock to the better land, however, he must lead them through some dangerous and dark ravines. On one side huge trees reach up to blot out the sun, making noontime as dark as twilight. On the other side of the ravine a deep precipice yawns in sheer descent to a riverbed where the water foams and roars, torn by jagged rocks. Hidden in the shadows in this dark pathway are dangers—serpents coiled to strike and wolves ready to pounce upon a sheep to destroy it. Yet the sheep go through this dangerous ravine of darkness because the shepherd has led them there!

What is true of a shepherd with his sheep is also true of the Saviour with the saint. For Christ, the Good Shepherd, knows full well that if we are going to go on to higher ground, we can only reach it by passing through places of difficulty. If you asked my children what they liked best about school, they would probably tell you recess. But of course if all of school were recess they would learn nothing at all. Most of us, like youngsters, enjoy romping on the playground of prosperity. But God knows that the only way that we can reach the higher places of Christian experience is to go through the schoolroom of suffering. When we come to these gloomy experiences in life, the Shepherd is with us. And if He leads us there, it is the right place for us to be. And if He is with us, we can take courage in His presence.

I am sure as David wrote this psalm he could remember how as a shepherd boy he had led his own flocks through the valley of darkness. He could hear the distant howl of the wolf or the hyena that lay in wait for his flock, and for the sheepherder too. David could remember how at such moments his sheep huddled close to his heels, and how he prepared to fight for their lives. Ask a shepherd of Palestine to show his arms and his feet, and you will see the scars he has received fighting the enemies of the flock. David had learned that the life of a man also had dangerous passages. But just as the sheep crept under his protection, so he had learned where to place his trust. He knew that when he came to the deep, dark valleys of life, he did not have to be afraid because he had a Shepherd to protect him and fight for him.

Where do you get your courage? Where do you get the stamina to stand up to life? For the psalmist, and for the Christian, courage does not come from whistling in the dark as though there were no evil in the dark valley. Nor does courage come from believing that we can defend ourselves. Obviously, as sheep we are helpless, and any fight in which we might engage would be a battle in the dark. Our courage comes from knowing that the events of our lives are under the control of God. Our bravery springs from trusting the presence of Christ our Shepherd.

What are you going through today? What shadows seem to lie across your tomorrows? The Shepherd knows them all, and you can be unafraid of the trip through the dark valley, if you trust Him. The Scriptures promise, "The Lord is at hand. Be careful for nothing [in nothing be anxious], but in everything by prayer and supplication with thanksgiving let your requests be made known unto God. And the peace of God, which passeth all understanding, shall keep [guard] your hearts and minds [thoughts] through Christ Jesus" (Phil. 4:5b-6).

WHEN THOU PASSEST THROUGH THE WATERS
(Isaiah 43:2)

Is there any heart discouraged as it journeys on its way?
    Does there seem to be more darkness than there is of sunny day?
Oh, it's hard to learn the lesson, as we pass beneath the rod,
    That the sunshine and the shadows serve alike the will of God.
But there comes a word of promise, like the promise of a bow,
    That however deep the waters they shall never overflow.

When the flesh is worn and weary, and the spirit is depressed,
    And temptations sweep upon it like a storm on the ocean's breast;
There's a haven ever open for the tempest-driven bird;
    There's a shelter for the tempted in the promise of the Word.
For the standard of the Spirit shall be raised against the foe,
    And however deep the waters they shall never overflow.

When a sorrow comes upon you that no other soul can share,
    And the burden seems too heavy for the human heart to bear;
There is One whose grace can comfort if you'll give Him an abode;
    There's a Burden Bearer ready, if you'll trust Him with your load.
For the precious promise reaches to the depths of human woe;
    That however deep the waters they shall never overflow.

When the sands of life are ebbing and I near the Jordan's shore,
    When I see its waters rising and hear its billows roar,
I will reach my hand to Jesus, in His bosom I will hide
    And 'twill only be a moment till I reach the other side.
It is then the fullest meaning of the promise I shall know:
    When thou passest through the waters they shall never overflow.

Selected

COURAGE TO TRUST

Probably the most familar verse in Psalm 23 is: "Yea, though I walk through the valley of the shadow of death, I will fear no evil: for thou art with me." It is familiar, I suppose, because it is usually quoted in times of sorrow and death. When the psalmist wrote these words, however, he probably was not thinking about death at all. He was talking about an actual place in Palestine, the valley of the shadows or "the valley of deep darkness."

Somewhere in the hills of Judah where David watched his flocks as a boy, there was a ravine through which the shepherd led his sheep. Darkness fell early, and wild beasts lay in wait for the flock. The shepherd would lead his sheep through this steep and narrow gorge in order to bring them to higher and greener pasture. It took courage for a sheep to follow the shepherd through this dangerous ravine and the sheep gained its courage by relying upon the shepherd. Its only safety lay in keeping close to the shepherd's side and in obeying his commands. What David is saying is that he had courage to go through the fearful experiences of life because he had a Shepherd who led him into those experiences and who would defend him from their dangers.

But whether the ancient poet intended it or not, it is not without significance that the experience has been translated for centuries "The valley of the shadow of death." Death is the darkest valley that lies before us. We are fearful when our loved ones go through it and more fearful when we face it ourselves. Fear of that journey has robbed many people of the joy and zest of life and has made them old. Of all our enemies, death is not only the last, it is the worst. In fact, Americans spend a great deal to fool themselves into thinking that they will not go through death. Age creeps on, but we fight to push it back. We turn to the hairdresser or the health club, to lotions and hair dyes in order to kid ourselves into thinking that life here can go on forever. We just will not face up to it. We disguise death with flowers and smother it with soft music. We play the game right to the end and put rouge on the corpse and talk inanely about "How alive he looks." We show our fear by not facing up to death. Yét David knew about the dark places of death and he was able to face it with courage.

Notice the interesting change of pronouns in the middle of Psalm 23. In the opening verses David has been talking *about* the Shepherd. But suddenly in verse 4 there is a change, and David begins to talk *to* the Shepherd. "Yea, though I walk through the valley of the shadow of death, I will fear no evil: for *thou* art with me." The psalmist has turned his song from praise to prayer. Perhaps David remembered the times when Saul, insane with jealousy, pursued him to the desert and would have taken his life. Perhaps he thought of the rebels who would have even then slain him in order to rob him of his throne. And when he felt the clammy hand of terror squeezing his heart, he wrote, "I won't be afraid, for *Thou* art with me!"

A little boy was crossing the United States on a transcontinental train. As little boys often do, he got rather restless and kept getting up for a drink of water. After a while his mother's nerves were worn thin and a woman across the aisle felt sorry for her. She called the little boy over and said, "My, you're a good looking little boy!" He smiled. She said, "That's a lovely sailor suit you have on." The youngster looked down and said, "My mommy made it. She sewed on the metal buttons, and she put on the stripes, and she put this buckle on the pants." Then as the youngster was telling the woman what his mother had done, the train went into a tunnel and the car was blanketed by darkness. The little boy left the woman to whom he was talking and running across the aisle he threw his arms around his mother and said, "Mommy, Mommy, you're here and I'm not scared, am I?" It was nice to talk about his mommy as long as things were in the sunshine, but when the darkness came he no longer talked *about* his mother, he talked *to* her. David was doing something like that. When he thought about the rest and refreshment and the sunny green pastures, he talked about his Shepherd. But when he thought about the dark spots in life through which he had passed and through which he was sure to go, he spoke directly to the Lord. "When I go through those places, *Thou* art with me!"

Someone asked John Wesley, the founder of Methodism, the secret of the movement's success. Wesley is said to have replied, "Our folks die well!" Sorrow and death can make the presence of Christ very real. Men and women who have placed their trust in Him know that He delivers them from the fear of death. When we think about death we recognize His personal presence and can say when we go through that dark valley, "Thou art with me!"

After all, Jesus Christ has gone through the valley of death Himself, and He has come out victorious on the other side. We can be certain that because He is with us He will do the same for us.

But the imagery of this verse stands for other experiences in life besides dying, for we often have to pass through dark valleys. If we are to have courage in these experiences we must appropriate the power of the Shepherd. What kind of courage does a sheep need? There is one kind of courage a sheep *does not* need: courage to fight its enemies. The most courageous sheep in the world would be an easy meal for the smallest wolf. But a sheep does need courage to trust the shepherd. When a mountain lion comes to attack the flock or a wolf lurks close by, the sheep needs only look up to be sure that the shepherd is near. Then it can go back to grazing. And that takes courage!

The most difficult lesson of the Christian life to learn is that you cannot fight spiritual battles by yourself. We are just helpless sheep, and unless the Shepherd defeats our enemies, we will be found someplace out in the desert of life, torn and bleeding. The frightening events of life should not be allowed to interrupt our grazing. Yet, when we become afraid we want to land some kind of knockout blow ourselves. Instead we must trust the Shepherd. We must turn the struggle over to His hand and go back to feeding again. That takes courage; but it also gives courage.

In Revelation the risen Christ, our Shepherd, says, "Fear not; I am the first and the last: I am he that liveth, and was dead; and, behold, I am alive for evermore, Amen; and have the keys of hell and of death" (Rev. 1:17b-18). This same Jesus Christ is waiting to come into your life today and to give you, through His presence, courage to live triumphantly here and in the hereafter.

STRONG YET TENDER

THE SCRIPTURES refer to sheep, lambs, ewes, sheepfolds and shepherds about six hundred times. God seems to be saying, "If you want to learn something about the Christian life, watch the sheep. And if you want to know something about Me, watch a faithful shepherd." As we have seen, the greatest king Israel ever knew, David, pictured his relationship with God as that of a sheep to a shepherd. David put himself in the position of a helpless, defenseless sheep when he wrote, "The LORD is my shepherd; I shall not want." As David's Shepherd God provided rest by making him lie down in green pastures; He supplied refreshment by leading him to still waters. God restored him when he wandered and He guided the psalmist into right paths. Even when David went through the valley of the shadow of death, he had courage because his Shepherd went with him. In verse 4 the psalmist declares that since he is God's sheep and God is his Shepherd, he would not lack for comfort, because "Thy rod and thy staff they *comfort* me."

The rod and the staff symbolized the shepherd's power. The "rod," a great oak club about two feet long, was used to defend the flock against wild beasts. The rod had a round head, usually whittled from the knot of a tree bough, in which the shepherd had pounded sharp bits of metal. A skillful shepherd not only swung the club to smash the head of an attacker but he could also hurl the club like a missile over the heads of his flock to strike a wolf lurking in the distance.

The shepherd's staff or crook was sometimes bent or hooked at one end. With the staff the shepherd restrained the sheep from wandering or hooked their legs to pull them out of holes into which they had fallen. He also used it to pull branches aside when a sheep got tangled in a thicket or to beat back the high grass to drive out serpents coiled in the path.

"Thy rod and thy staff they comfort me." The sheep takes comfort from the Shepherd's power. In fact the word *comfort* all through the Scriptures means "with strength." To comfort is to give strength by supplying power. We have diluted the word so that with us it is just a way of speaking. We say, "Cheer up, things will get better" to comfort someone when deep inside we are sure they will not. We use words to smooth and quiet and calm.

God offers His people more than a pocket handkerchief to dry their tears—He offers them His power and His might. Frankly, we tend to be a bit afraid of God's power. Usually it fills us with awe—but not with comfort. Perhaps this comes about because when we were enemies of God, we shuddered to think of falling into God's hands. Enemies of the flock usually fear the shepherd's rod. Or perhaps we are afraid of God's power because we think that God is very much like ourselves. We are unpredictable. One day we are up and the next day we are down. One day we are bathed in smiles and another we sink into a mood. At times we insist that "we are not ourselves today" implying, of course, that we are really somebody else. We suspect that God is that way. Sometimes He uses His power on our behalf but on other days He wants to flex His muscle a bit and like the gods of the ancient Greeks, hurls a thunderbolt into our lives. Naturally, if God used His might like *that* it would bring anything but comfort—it would fill us with fear.

But our Shepherd is as tender as He is powerful. God cannot use His power outside of His love. Our God is the most self-obligated Being in the universe. His grace limits His power just as His holiness limits His love. God will not move in might except to carry out the desires of His heart. It is the power and the affection of the Shepherd found in the phrase "*Thy* rod and *thy* staff" that bring comfort to His flock. They know that these weapons will only be used in their defense.

Several years ago our daughter almost died. One evening she suddenly became very ill. When the doctor examined her, he rushed her to the hospital. He told me that he was not sure whether she would live through the night. I remember standing in the dimly lit hospital room and watching helplessly as our little girl struggled for her life. In those moments some great truths of Scripture came to my mind. First of all, I knew that God loved us and that He loved our little child. After all, He loved us enough to die for us. I knew, therefore, that God desired only our highest good. But I loved my little girl too, and I was helpless to do what my love desired. Then I realized that the God who loved us was also the God of power. I knew that He had the strength to do what love dictated. If God chose that our daughter stay with us, He had the power to keep her alive.

I knew, therefore, that if God chose to take our daughter from us that this too was a loving choice. He had the power to do anything that His heart knew best. If she went to be with Him in heaven, it would be the very best thing for her and for us. My love was limited, but God's love was not. In that midnight hour I knew something of the comfort of God, comfort that dries our tears and calms our fears because we can rest our lives in God's strength.

Would it really comfort us if all our "why's" were answered? Why the child had to meet that deadly virus? Why the road was wet just then, and why you were on the curve at the fatal moment? If God simply gave us answers—scientific, philosophical explanations for all our bruising questions—could they comfort us? A child is not comforted by being told just why his toy broke, or why his finger hurts when it is bruised in a car door, or why his tummy aches. But he is comforted by knowing that his mother loves him, and that she can do something about his hurt.

From the defending rod and staff of our Shepherd we can derive abundant comfort, not only for ourselves but also for others. You can comfort others by sharing with them the power that God has displayed in helping you. Paul writes, "Blessed be God, even the Father of our Lord Jesus Christ, the Father of mercies and the God of all comfort; who comforteth us in all our tribulation, that we may be able to comfort them which are in any trouble, by the comfort wherewith we ourselves are comforted of God" (II Cor. 1:3-4).

OIL OF PROTECTION

It is a dangerous venture to live in the twentieth century! Browse through the newspaper and you are bombarded with accounts of car accidents, plane crashes and murders. We all live looking down the barrel of an atomic shotgun. Physical dangers are not the worst. Man has built bridges, erected tall buildings and designed atomic transportation. In such a society, it is easy to feel that God has retired—that we do not need Him anymore. That situation is filled with spiritual dangers.

Yet, it has always been dangerous to be alive. In other days men were stricken with pestilence and diseases that we do not face now. And this world has never been much of a friend to God and to His people. Three thousand years ago when David wrote about his life with God in Psalm 23 he said, "Thou preparest a table before me in the presence of mine enemies: thou anointest my head with oil." He said that if the Lord was his Shepherd and he was His sheep, he would not want for protection.

Some commentators have suggested that the Twenty-third Psalm changes between verses 4 and 5 from a description of sheep with the shepherd to a banquet prepared by a host for a friend. But I think that here, too, David has in mind a picture of shepherd life in Palestine. Charles W. Slemming, who has written a great deal about shepherds in the Middle East, tells of one such experience when a shepherd comes to a new field in which to feed his flock. He inspects the field closely, walking up and down the field looking for grass that could poison the sheep. He also inspects the field for vipers. These tiny brown adders live under the ground, and they have a way of popping up out of their small holes and nipping the noses of the sheep. Their bite is poisonous and sometimes the inflammation from their bite will kill the sheep.

The shepherd leaves the sheep outside any such infested field. Then he walks up and down the field until he finds vipers' holes. He takes from his girdle a bottle of thick oil. Then, raking over any long grass with his staff, he pours a circle of oil at the top of every viper's hole he can find. As he leads the sheep into the field, he anoints the head of each sheep with the oil. When the vipers beneath the ground realize that the sheep are grazing above, they come out of their holes to do their deadly damage. But the oil keeps them from getting out. The smooth bodies of the vipers cannot pass over the slippery oil—and they are prisoners inside their holes.

Moreover, the oil on the sheep's head acts as a repellent, so if a viper gets near the nose of the sheep the smell drives the viper away. Literally, therefore, the sheep are allowed to graze in plenty in the presence of their enemies. What the shepherd did for the sheep, God does for His people. If you are a Christian, God has sent you to live in a dangerous place. Remember in Matthew 10:16 that our Lord said to His disciples, "I send you forth as sheep in the midst of wolves." The most dangerous place for a sheep to be is in the midst of a wolf pack. God sends His sheep to live in the no-man's-land between the safety of the church and the dangers of the world. Some Christians refuse to follow the Shepherd to this dangerous field.

For many the Christian life consists of worship services, religious meetings and going to social events at the church. Such people appear very religious, but they may be disobedient. Jesus Christ sent us into the *world*—into our society—to live for Him there. He said, "I pray not that thou shouldest take them out of the world, but that thou shouldest keep them from the evil. They are not of the world, even as I am not of the world. Sanctify [set apart] them in thy truth: thy word is truth" (John 17:15-17). Christ specifically said that He did not want Christians taken out of the world—He only prayed that they would be protected from evil.

What was our Lord's relationship to the world? He spent time with sinners. He cultivated their friendship. Again and again the Pharisees attacked Him for eating with publicans and sinners. Ultimately they crucified Him because He spent time with needy people. As He was related to the world, we are to be related to the world. Anyone can live an acceptable Christian life within the confines of a church. But it takes the power of God to live that life in a world that is opposed to Jesus Christ. Yet that is just what Christ expects of us. We are the light of the world—but light is useless unless it comes in contact with darkness. Paul says that we are "letters to be seen and read of all men."

One reason that we fail to cultivate the friendship of unbelievers is that we are afraid. We do not have them to our home for dinner or see them socially because we feel that their values could become our values and instead of wolves becoming sheep the sheep could be devoured by the wolf pack. It is too dangerous. Yet that is just where Christ called us to go. We are not to be *isolated* from sinners—we are to be separate in that we are distinct and different from them.

Notice in John 17 the Lord prays, "Sanctify them through thy truth." The word "sanctify" simply means "set them apart." Our Lord is praying, "Set them apart through Bible study." It is as we study the Scriptures and appropriate the provision that God has made for our protection that we can graze in dangerous pastures, yet dwell in spiritual safety. God has given us the Holy Spirit—a Person to guard us; God has given us His Word—principles to guide us.

In the Great Commission (Matt. 28:18-20), "Go ye therefore, and teach all nations," have you ever wondered what the word "therefore" is there for? In the previous verse Christ said, "All power is given unto me in heaven and in earth." Then He declared, "Lo, I am with you alway." He gives us His authority to be in the world and His presence to protect us. It is dangerous to live amid enemies. But God directs us to dangerous spots and it is there that He feeds us. You are far safer in such a place with God than you could possibly be anywhere else without Him.

People all around us need to feed where we feed. They need to know the kindness of our Shepherd and live their lives under His care. If we do not go where He has sent us, they may never see what Christ can do in human lives.

HIS LAVISH BOUNTY

COMPLAINING can develop into a fine art! Some tarnished souls can look at any situation and tell you what is wrong with it. Such people are "walking minus signs." Unfortunately, a few of these sour spirits have joined our churches. They look as though they sucked lemons for breakfast. One of these saints is said to have lived complaining and died complaining. When he finally got to heaven, his first comment was, "The halo don't fit!"

When you meet these people you know they are poverty stricken. I do not mean that they do not have money. They often do. But though they may have fat purses, they have lean souls. Christians who sing the song of heaven in a minor key do not impress others with the richness of their faith. The people who convince me of the reality of Jesus Christ are those sturdy saints who sing with the psalmist, "My cup runneth over."

Of course, David knew hard times. His son Absalom had been guilty of treason; Ahithophel, his adviser, betrayed him; Joab, his army chief, deserted him. His wife scolded him for his humility; Adonijah, a favorite son, tried to steal his throne. The former king, Saul, had made him an enemy without a cause. If David had wanted to complain, he could have kept us up all night. But David had learned to trust his life to the Lord. He found that *God* never failed him and that God's provision for his life was poured from an overflowing cup. That is why David could sound a note of joy in this psalm.

David's image here is not of someone spilling water in his lap. He was thinking of the care and consideration of a faithful shepherd for his sheep. Sometimes a shepherd found a very deep well from which to draw water for his flock. Many were a hundred feet down to the water. To draw the water the shepherd used a long rope with a leather bucket at the end. The bucket held only three quarts. It had to be let down and drawn up hand over hand and the water poured into large stone cups beside the well. It was a long, laborious process! If a shepherd had a hundred sheep and the well was deep, he might have to draw for two hours if he allowed the sheep to drink all they wished. Sheep do not like to get wet, and it was a mark of special kindness to keep the cups filled to the brim so that they could drink with ease.

Here is where the hireling shepherd displayed his heartlessness. As soon as a sheep had only half enough water, he would shove it aside to keep from having to draw more water. But the Shepherd of the psalmist had no such disposition. He drew and drew and filled the cups to overflowing. He was untiring in His efforts to satisfy the thirsty sheep.

Our God is a great Giver! He is lavish in His bounties to us. He not only gives us what we ask or think; He gives us *exceeding abundantly* above all that we ask or think (Eph. 3:20).

With Him the calf is always the fatted calf; the robe is always the best robe; the joy is unspeakable; and the peace passes understanding. There is no grudging in God's goodness. He does not measure His goodness by drops like a druggist filling a prescription. It comes to us in floods. If only we recognized the lavish abundance of His gifts, what a difference it would make in our lives! If every meal were taken as a gift from His hand, it would be almost a sacrament.

Has there ever been a time in your life when you did not know where the next meal was coming from? At the last moment God provided a bowl of soup and a bit of bread. And we were thankful —very, very thankful for what the Lord had provided. But when He supplies food for us so that we have to count calories to keep from eating too much, we sit down at the table and with little more than an unthinking word of thanks we complain about how difficult the day was. We just do not live in the light of His goodness, and our souls shrivel up.

God not only provides an abundance of goods for us, but He is abundant in His pardon. That is the glad message of the Bible. Yet we take God's forgiveness for granted. As H. G. Wells once remarked, "Forgiveness? Of course, God forgives—that's His business."

Dwight L. Moody, the famous evangelist, spoke at a penitentiary in Canon City, Colorado, on Thanksgiving Day, 1899. When the governor of the state heard that Moody would be at the prison he wrote to him, enclosing a pardon for a woman who had served three years of a ten-year sentence. At the close of his address, Moody produced the pardon, saying, "I have a pardon in my hands for one of the prisoners before me." He had intended to say something more, but he saw the strain caused by his announcement was so severe that he dared not go on. Calling the woman's name, he asked her to come forward to accept the governor's Thanksgiving gift.

The woman hesitated a moment, then got up, uttering a shriek, and, crossing her arms over her breast, fell sobbing and laughing across the lap of the woman next to her. The excitement was so intense that Moody could do nothing more than to make a brief application of the scene to illustrate God's offer of pardon and peace. Afterward Moody observed that if anyone showed such interest or excitement during his meetings after accepting the pardon offered for all sin, he would be labeled as a fanatic. We prize more highly the pardon of a fellowman than the abundant pardon of our God.

It is not the way of God only to save you but to save you fully—overflowingly. My cup overflows because of who Jesus Christ is and what He does. Look at what He will do for you when you trust your life into His hands.

He directs your day.
He helps you carry out His plan.
He makes your life a green pasture—not a barren, rock-strewn field.
He refreshes you in the dreary grind of life.
He puts you at rest regarding your eternal destiny.
He puts you at rest as to a purpose in your life.
He restores your soul in spite of the way you have pushed Him out of your life.
He takes away from you the fear of your own death.
He comforts you with His presence and His power.
He protects you from the dangers of life and provides for your daily needs.

Count your blessings, name them one by one. It is little wonder that John Welch of Scotland cried when thinking of God's blessings, "Oh, Lord, hold Thy hand, it is enough: Thy servant is a clay vessel and can contain no more!"

PARDON AND BLESSING

Satchel Paige was one of the best pitchers to ever throw a baseball, and also one of the oldest. Someone asked Satchel the secret of his long life and happy outlook and he replied, "Well, I never look behind me—'cause you can never tell who's comin' up and gaining you." If I understand him correctly, Paige was saying, "Don't think about tomorrow because it may be filled with trouble." Now that is not bad advice. Some people spend their lives worrying about all of the horrible things that may happen tomorrow. Worrying becomes a hobby.

If your only thoughts of the future are filled with worry, it would be wiser not to think about what is coming. Your tomorrows are actually ruining your todays. But there is an even better way to handle your tomorrows than to ignore them. That is to place your future in the hands of God.

The Psalmist David did not mind looking to the days ahead. He confidently asserted, "Surely goodness and mercy shall follow me all the days of my life." David had lived a full life with God. He had felt the rage of battle and heard the acclaim of the nations. He had climbed to the heights and fallen to the depths. Few lives have so much of life crowded in.

In Psalm 23 David reviewed his experience with God who had given him rest by making him to lie down in green pastures and refreshing him beside still waters. David had been restored when wandering, and guided into right paths. God's courage had come to him in the dark valleys and His comfort had blanketed him in dangerous places. He had been protected from enemies and made to drink from an overflowing cup.

In this final verse the psalmist passes from his past experiences to his present and future life with God. David's past experience with God gives birth to hope. David had seen God's faithfulness in the varying circumstances through the years and, because of that, he had hope for the years to come. After the thrills and dangers of the first five verses, still it was God's goodness and mercy that occupied David's thoughts.

Notice that God sends goodness and mercy. Not goodness alone, for we are sinners needing forgiveness; not mercy alone, for we need many things besides forgiveness. But they are linked to each other.

Goodness is getting those things that we do not deserve. Mercy is withholding those things we do deserve. Goodness to provide; mercy to pardon. David often joined these two together as when he declared, "The LORD is good; his mercy is everlasting." The goodness of God is found in immeasurable abundance and it touches every part of our lives. There is not a material and a spiritual side to a Christian's life. The religion of the Bible is a practical, down-to-earth affair! Jesus taught that God knows about the doctor bill, the visit to the dentist—and that we who trust a good God can be sure that He will provide for those basic necessities of life. You know this to be true if you have walked with the Shepherd in the past and have seen all that He has done for you.

It is astounding how different life can become when you recognize the goodness of God. Of course there will be many events that you will not be able to explain, but you can go through them triumphantly when you realize that your days are ordered by a good God. There are things which you will desire that a good God cannot let you have. You do not give a child poison to play with no matter how much he begs for it—not if you are a good parent. You do not keep a child home from school because he does not want to go—not if you are a good parent. You do what is best even when the youngster cannot understand.

David is not saying that all kinds of special good things will come into his life—to make him a spoiled child. The kindness of God is not kindness as a child may view it—what I want whenever I want it. Instead, it is the bringing of the Christian through those events in life which mold him to be more like Christ.

The Apostle Paul in Romans 8:28 declares, "All things work together for good to them that love God, to them who are the called according to his purpose." Does this mean that cancer is "good" and we should be happy for it? Of course not. It means that God works through these things so that together they help us to fit into His plan. A housewife puts a great many different ingredients into a cake. No one in his right mind would say that the ingredients all taste good—some would be difficult to swallow by themselves. Yet in the hand of a competent housewife the bitter and sweet are blended together into a delicious cake. So the Good Shepherd orders the events of our lives so that we will ultimately become what He wants us to be.

The psalmist was also sure that *mercy* would follow him. This loving-kindness of God includes His compassion, patience, forgiveness and help. All that God is glorified to bestow we are blessed to receive. How much we need God's mercy! How black is our sin and how foul our disobedience—yet there is mercy! When the Russian spies, the Rosenburgs, were tried in court for their treason against the United States, the trial was a long and bitter one. Judge Kauffman, who tried the case, was one of the most insulted and mistreated men in America. During the final sentence the lawyer for the Rosenburgs cried, "Your Honor, what my clients ask for is justice!" Judge Kauffman replied, "What the court has given you is what you ask for—justice! What you really want is mercy—but that is something this court has no right to give you."

The Judge of all the earth has a cause against us when we sin, and if *He* gives us justice we will be lost forever. Any one of my sins would shut me off from God just as darkness is destroyed in the presence of light. But God is merciful. Through the death of Jesus Christ who paid the penalty for all my sins, God acts in mercy. The blood of Jesus Christ allows Him to provide forgiveness and cleansing. I do not have to fear the future because I know that nothing—neither my circumstances nor my sin—shall separate me from Jesus Christ, my Shepherd. He who has been faithful in the past will continue faithful until the end.

Surely goodness and mercy will pursue me. *Surely*—because God has never failed me in the past. *Surely*—because He does not begin a work He does not complete. *Surely*—because the united testimony of all of His saints attests with David that He never fails nor forsakes. If the Lord is your Shepherd and you are His sheep, you will not want for goodness and mercy. Surely, they will follow you all the days of your life.

SAFELY HOME FOREVER

If someone were to ask, "What is a Christian?" what would you say? When a little boy asked that question, his father described a Christian by the church he went to, the wonderful life he lived, the goals he had. When he was finished, the little boy looked up and said, "Daddy, have I ever *seen* a Christian?"

Think a minute then. Simply and clearly, what *is* a Christian? Sometime ago an interviewer asked Phillip Wylie, the noted author, whether he classified himself as a Christian. Wylie replied, "I wouldn't be that arrogant!" You cannot help but wonder how Wylie would have defined a Christian. But what about *you*? How would you describe a Christian? Would you start by telling me about the organization he belongs to? Would you begin by describing the good life he lived? Or perhaps you would tell me about the facts that he believes.

Of course Christians do attend church. They do live different kinds of lives—or they should. Christians do believe certain important facts. But essentially Christianity is not any of those things. Christianity is a relationship with the person of Jesus Christ. It is interesting to note that in Psalm 23 David is talking about his personal relationship with God. He is saying that if the Lord is your Shepherd and you are His sheep you will not want for anything at any time. His Shepherd has provided rest and refreshment, restoration and guidance, courage and comfort, protection and provision. What is more, David looked to the future in the happy confidence that goodness and mercy would follow him like sheep dogs and that he himself would dwell in the house of the Lord forever.

Now all of these things that the Shepherd *does* will thrill the heart, but you will have missed the meaning of the psalm completely unless you understand that David is singing about his personal, intimate relationship with God. Notice how David ends this psalm —"I will dwell in the house of the Lord for ever." Most people read those words and immediately think of heaven. What a wonderful place that will be. I am confident though that David is not thinking precisely of where he would be but with whom he would be.

In Psalm 27:4 David declared, "One thing have I asked of the LORD, that will I seek after; that I may dwell in the house of the LORD all the days of my life, to behold the beauty of the LORD, and to enquire in his temple." David wanted to be in the Lord's house because then he could be in the Lord's presence. Whatever heaven is, it is primarily a place where we will be with Christ. Our family owns a comfortable house, and after I have been on a trip I enjoy coming home. Motels may have nicer furniture, they may have a great deal of service to offer their guests and the managers may try to make their guests feel "at home," but they never quite do. Home is home primarily because my wife and children are there. Take them away and our house becomes a dreary place.

Just before our Lord left the earth He told His disciples, "Let not your heart be troubled . . . I go to prepare a place for you, and if I go . . . I will come again and receive you unto myself; that where I am, there you may be also" (John 14:1-3). These words brushed away their tears because they had the promise of being with Him. We who are Christ's sheep can be sure that Jesus Christ who had led us safely through life will see us to His fold. Our Shepherd will not throw us into some ditch of a grave and forget us. He will take us to be with Himself on the other side.

Dr. G. Campbell Morgan tells of an incident that took place while he was a pastor in London. A young girl from his church lay dying. She had given birth to a child, and it appeared that it would cost her her life. Dr. Morgan went to visit the girl and stood back in the shadow of her room while the doctor did his best to take care of her. She was delirious and kept saying, "Doctor, I don't want to go on alone. Doctor, please, I want to take my baby with me."

The doctor tried to say something that would help her. "My dear, your baby will have loving care—you need not be afraid. You can't take the baby with you. The gate through which you must go is only wide enough for one." Campbell Morgan stepped forward and touched the physician's shoulder and said, "Doctor, don't tell her that! Tell her that the gate through which she is about to pass is wide enough for *two*—for herself and for her Shepherd. He who has brought her to this place will not desert her now, but He'll see her safely home to the other side!"

Psalm 23 begins and ends with God. "The LORD is my shepherd . . . I will dwell in the house of the LORD for ever." The psalm means nothing without *Him*. Christianity begins and ends with

Jesus Christ. You become a Christian by knowing Him personally, and the prospect of the Christian is to dwell with Him for all eternity. Do you know Him? I am not asking whether you know *about* Him. Thousands of people brought up in Sunday school know all of the facts, but they do not know Him. I do not mean, do you know the *psalm*? Scores of people can recite this psalm who do not know the Shepherd. Do you know Him? I do not mean, do you appreciate the poetry of this ancient song? But do you know the Shepherd? Jesus Christ calls you to Himself. "Come unto me all ye that labour and are heavy laden, and I will give you rest" (Matt. 11:28). "Whosoever believeth in him should not perish, but have everlasting life" (John 3:16b). "As many as received him, to them gave he power to become the sons of God" (John 1:12).

Probably the most important single word in this psalm is the little word *my*. You can know that the Lord is a Shepherd but that will not do you much good. You can even understand that the Lord is *the* Shepherd—the only One in the universe who can fully meet your need. It is only when you have come to place your confidence in Him personally that you can sing with David of old, "The LORD is *my* shepherd, I shall not want." It is then that you can affirm with the conviction based on God's promise, "I *will* dwell in the house of the Lord for ever."

Moody Press, a ministry of the Moody Bible Institute, is designed for education, evangelization and edification. If we may assist you in knowing more about Christ and the Christian life, please write us without obligation to: Moody Press, c/o MLM, Chicago, Illinois 60610.

Cover colorphoto by Fred Sieb
Interior photographs by H. Armstrong Roberts